Dear Consumer:

How to Escape Debt and Everyday Spending

Sara J Dashning

Dear Consumer: How to Escape Debt and Everyday Spending | Sara J Dashning© 2024

"Dear Consumer: How to Escape Debt and Everyday Spending" is an empowering guide that unveils the hidden traps of consumer culture and provides actionable steps for reclaiming financial freedom. In a world where excessive consumption reigns, this book offers a roadmap for breaking free from the cycle of endless spending. By shedding light on the pervasive influences that drive unnecessary purchases, readers will gain a deeper understanding of their own consumer behaviors. From practical budgeting techniques to mindfulness strategies, "Dear Consumer" equips readers with the tools they need to take control of their finances and live a more intentional life. It's time to step off the treadmill of consumerism and embrace a future of financial stability and fulfillment.

Understanding the Consumer Culture Trap

In the bustling landscape of modern society, we find ourselves ensnared within the intricate web of consumer culture—a labyrinthine construct designed to tantalize, seduce, and ultimately ensnare even the most discerning individuals. But how did we arrive at this juncture, where the pursuit of material possessions has become synonymous with happiness and fulfillment?

To truly comprehend the depths of the consumer culture trap, we must delve into the annals of human psychology. From the earliest days of our existence, humans have been hardwired to seek out sources of pleasure and satisfaction. Our primal instincts drive us to acquire resources that fulfill our basic needs for survival. Yet, as civilization progressed and societies evolved, so too did our desires.

Enter the era of consumerism—a phenomenon propelled by the relentless march of industrialization and the advent of mass production. Suddenly, goods once considered luxuries became accessible to the masses, fueling a voracious appetite for consumption. Advertisers seized upon this burgeoning market, weaving intricate narratives of desire and aspiration around their products. Through clever marketing tactics and persuasive messaging, they transformed mundane objects into symbols of status and success.

But perhaps the most insidious aspect of the consumer culture trap lies in its ability to exploit our innate vulnerabilities. In a world inundated with endless choices and temptations, our brains are bombarded with stimuli, triggering a cascade of emotions and impulses. The fear of missing out (FOMO), the allure of instant gratification, and the relentless pursuit of social validation conspire to keep us locked in a perpetual cycle of consumption.

Yet, despite the superficial allure of material possessions, the consequences of our collective obsession with consumption are far-reaching and profound. From mounting debt burdens to environmental degradation, the toll exacted by our insatiable appetite for more is evident on both individual and societal levels.

As we embark on this journey to unravel the intricacies of the consumer culture trap, it is imperative that we confront these uncomfortable truths head-on. Only by understanding the forces that compel us to consume can we hope to break free from their grip and reclaim control over our lives. For in the pursuit of true happiness and fulfillment, the path to liberation begins with a single, audacious act—questioning the very foundations of the world we inhabit.

Why Escaping Debt and Spending Matters

In a world awash with abundance, one might wonder why escaping debt and curbing spending habits should rank among our highest priorities. After all, is not the pursuit of material wealth and comfort the cornerstone of the American Dream?

Yet, beneath the glossy veneer of consumer culture lies a stark reality—one marred by the debilitating effects of financial insecurity and indebtedness. For millions of individuals across the globe, the burden of debt serves as a constant source of stress and anxiety, eroding their quality of life and impeding their pursuit of happiness.

But the ramifications of our collective addiction to consumption extend far beyond the confines of personal finance. As we squander our resources on frivolous indulgences, we turn a blind eye to the pressing challenges facing our planet. From climate change to resource depletion, the environmental toll exacted by our insatiable appetite for more is nothing short of catastrophic.

Moreover, the relentless pursuit of material possessions exacts a heavy toll on our mental and emotional well-being. Caught in the relentless cycle of comparison and competition, we sacrifice our authenticity and sense of self-worth at the altar of consumerism. The pursuit of external validation becomes a Sisyphean task, forever out of reach yet tantalizingly close.

In light of these sobering realities, it becomes abundantly clear why escaping debt and everyday spending matters now more than ever. It is not merely a matter of financial prudence or personal responsibility, but rather a moral imperative—a call to action to reassess our values and priorities as individuals and as a society.

Yet, the path to financial liberation is fraught with challenges and obstacles, requiring courage, determination, and unwavering resolve. It demands that we challenge the status quo, question the narratives that society imposes upon us, and chart a course that aligns with our deepest aspirations and values.

As we embark on this journey together, let us heed the call to arms and take a stand against the forces that seek to imprison us within the confines of consumer culture. For in the pursuit of true freedom and fulfillment, the power to transform lies within each and every one of us. It is time to break free from the shackles of debt and excess and reclaim our rightful place as architects of our own destiny.

As we navigate the complexities of modern life, it's essential to recognize the profound impact that our financial decisions have on our overall well-being. Escaping debt and reigning in our spending habits isn't just about achieving financial stability—it's about reclaiming our autonomy, preserving our mental health, and safeguarding the planet for future generations.

First and foremost, the burden of debt exacts a heavy toll on our mental and emotional health. Studies have shown that individuals grappling with debt are more likely to experience symptoms of depression, anxiety, and stress. The constant worry about making ends meet and the shame associated with financial struggles can take a significant toll on our self-esteem and overall quality of life. Escaping debt isn't just a matter of dollars and cents—it's a crucial step towards preserving our mental well-being and regaining a sense of control over our lives.

Moreover, excessive spending isn't just harmful to our own financial health—it's also detrimental to the broader economy and environment. In a society driven by consumerism, our relentless pursuit of more has led to rampant overconsumption and resource depletion. From overflowing landfills to polluted oceans, the environmental consequences of our insatiable appetite for stuff are impossible to ignore. By scaling back our consumption and embracing more sustainable lifestyles, we can reduce our ecological footprint and pave the way for a healthier, more equitable world.

But perhaps most importantly, escaping debt and reevaluating our spending habits is an act of rebellion against the pervasive narratives of consumer culture. In a society that equates material possessions with happiness and success, choosing to prioritize financial freedom and fulfillment over mindless consumption is a radical act of defiance. It's a rejection of the notion that our worth is determined by the things we own and a reaffirmation of our intrinsic value as human beings.

By freeing ourselves from the shackles of debt and excess, we create space for the things that truly matter—authentic connections, meaningful experiences, and a sense of purpose that transcends material wealth. We reclaim our agency and autonomy, no longer beholden to the whims of advertisers or societal expectations. And in doing so, we pave the way for a more compassionate, sustainable future—one where our collective well-being takes precedence over profit margins and conspicuous consumption.

In the pages that follow, we'll explore practical strategies for escaping debt, curbing spending, and cultivating a more mindful approach to consumption. From budgeting tips to mindfulness exercises, we'll provide you with the tools and resources you need to take control of your finances and chart a course towards financial freedom. But more than that, we'll invite you to question the underlying assumptions and values that drive our consumerist culture and imagine a world where happiness isn't measured in dollars and cents.

So join us on this journey as we embark on a quest to reclaim our humanity and redefine our relationship with money. Together, we can break free from the shackles of debt and excess and build a brighter, more equitable future for ourselves and generations to come.

The Psychology of Consumer Behavior

What drives us to open our wallets and part with our hard-earned cash? It's a question that has puzzled economists, psychologists, and marketers alike for decades. Yet, at its core, the answer lies in the complex interplay of human psychology and our innate desires for connection, status, and security.

At the heart of consumer behavior lies a fundamental truth: we are social creatures, hardwired to seek out acceptance and belonging within our communities. From the earliest days of our evolution, our survival depended on our ability to cooperate and collaborate with others. In today's hyper-connected world, this primal urge manifests itself in our relentless pursuit of status symbols and material possessions.

Consider, for instance, the phenomenon of conspicuous consumption—the tendency to flaunt one's wealth and status through extravagant purchases. From luxury cars to designer handbags, these symbols of affluence serve as tangible markers of social standing, signaling to others our success and prestige. But beneath the surface lies a deeper psychological truth: our propensity for conspicuous consumption is driven not by a desire for material goods per se, but rather by a need for validation and approval from our peers.

This need for social approval extends beyond material possessions to encompass our consumption habits more broadly. Studies have shown that we are more likely to purchase products and services that are endorsed by others or associated with desirable social groups. From celebrity endorsements to influencer marketing, advertisers leverage our innate desire to fit in and be accepted to persuade us to buy their products.

But perhaps the most powerful driver of consumer behavior is our insatiable appetite for novelty and excitement. In a world saturated with stimuli, we are constantly seeking out new experiences and sensations to stave off boredom and monotony. From the latest gadgets to trendy restaurants, our consumption habits are driven not just by a desire for utility, but by a craving for novelty and excitement.

Understanding the psychology of consumer behavior is essential if we are to break free from the grip of consumerism and reclaim control over our lives. By recognizing the underlying motives and impulses that drive our spending habits, we can begin to cultivate a more mindful and intentional approach to consumption. In the pages that follow, we'll explore practical strategies for navigating the complex landscape of consumer culture and forging a path towards financial freedom and fulfillment.

The Influence of Marketing and Advertising

In the age of information overload, advertisers face an uphill battle for our attention. With countless messages bombarding us from every direction, it's no wonder that marketers have become increasingly adept at capturing our interest and persuading us to part with our hard-earned cash.

At the heart of their arsenal lies the art of persuasion—a subtle and nuanced craft that seeks to influence our thoughts, feelings, and behaviors without our conscious awareness. From catchy jingles to eye-catching visuals, advertisers employ a myriad of tactics to capture our attention and elicit an emotional response.

But perhaps the most powerful tool in the marketer's arsenal is the power of suggestion. By tapping into our subconscious desires and fears, advertisers are able to subtly shape our perceptions and beliefs, guiding us towards their products and services with ease. Whether it's through clever product placement in movies and TV shows or targeted advertising on social media, they are able to infiltrate our consciousness and influence our purchasing decisions without us even realizing it.

Yet, for all their ingenuity, marketers are not infallible. In recent years, consumers have become increasingly skeptical of traditional advertising tactics, recognizing them for what they truly are—manipulative attempts to exploit our vulnerabilities for profit. As a result, advertisers have been forced to adapt their strategies, embracing more transparent and authentic approaches to marketing.

But make no mistake: the influence of marketing and advertising remains a potent force in our lives, shaping our perceptions, attitudes, and behaviors in ways both subtle and profound. If we are to break free from the grip of consumerism and reclaim control over our lives, we must remain vigilant against the insidious influence of advertising and cultivate a more critical and discerning approach to the media we consume.

In the pages that follow, we'll delve deeper into the psychology of advertising and explore practical strategies for resisting its influence. From mindfulness techniques to media literacy skills, we'll provide you with the tools and resources you need to navigate the complex landscape of modern marketing and make informed choices that align with your values and aspirations.

In today's hyper-connected world, the pervasive influence of social media has fundamentally altered the way we perceive ourselves and others. From carefully curated Instagram feeds to envy-inducing Facebook updates, we are bombarded with idealized images of perfection and success at every turn. Yet, beneath the surface lies a darker truth—a world of comparison, insecurity, and relentless self-doubt.

At the heart of this phenomenon lies the insidious force known as social comparison—a natural human tendency to evaluate ourselves in relation to others. In the context of social media, this tendency is magnified tenfold, as we are constantly bombarded with images of friends, acquaintances, and celebrities living seemingly perfect lives. Whether it's the latest vacation photos or glamorous party snapshots, these idealized images serve as constant reminders of our own inadequacies and shortcomings.

But perhaps even more insidious than social comparison itself is the fear of missing out (FOMO)— a pervasive sense of anxiety and insecurity triggered by the belief that others are experiencing more exciting and fulfilling lives than our own. In a world where every moment is documented and shared online, the pressure to keep up with the seemingly endless stream of social events and activities can feel overwhelming. Yet, paradoxically, the more we strive to keep pace with others, the more isolated and disconnected we ultimately become.

The impact of social comparison and FOMO extends far beyond the realm of our mental and emotional well-being, shaping our consumption habits and financial decisions in profound ways. Studies have shown that individuals who are prone to FOMO are more likely to engage in impulse buying and overspending, seeking to fill the void of insecurity and inadequacy with material possessions. Moreover, the constant barrage of aspirational images and lifestyles depicted on social media can foster a culture of conspicuous consumption, driving us to spend beyond our means in pursuit of an unattainable ideal.

But there is hope. By recognizing the destructive impact of social comparison and FOMO on our lives, we can begin to take proactive steps to mitigate their influence and reclaim control over our thoughts and actions. From cultivating gratitude and contentment to embracing a more minimalist lifestyle, there are countless strategies we can employ to cultivate a healthier relationship with social media and consumer culture.

In the pages that follow, we'll delve deeper into the psychological mechanisms underlying social comparison and FOMO, exploring practical strategies for overcoming their grip and reclaiming control over our lives. From mindfulness techniques to social media detoxes, we'll provide you with the tools and resources you need to break free from the cycle of comparison and cultivate a more meaningful and fulfilling existence.

So join us on this journey as we unravel the complexities of social comparison and FOMO and chart a course towards a future defined not by external validation and material wealth, but by inner peace, contentment, and authentic connection.

Facing the Reality of Debt

In the labyrinth of modern finance, few specters loom as large or as menacing as the burden of debt. For millions of individuals across the globe, debt is not just a financial inconvenience—it's a constant source of stress, anxiety, and shame. Yet, in order to break free from its suffocating grasp, we must first confront the stark reality of our financial situation head-on.

The journey begins with a sobering assessment of our debts—a task that requires both courage and honesty. Whether it's credit card balances, student loans, or mortgages, each debt represents a weighty burden that must be acknowledged and addressed. Yet, far too often, we shy away from confronting these uncomfortable truths, burying our heads in the sand and hoping that our financial woes will simply disappear.

But the harsh reality is that debt, left unchecked, has a way of multiplying and metastasizing, wreaking havoc on our financial well-being and undermining our hopes for the future. From high interest rates to late fees and penalties, the costs of carrying debt can quickly spiral out of control, trapping us in a vicious cycle of borrowing and repayment.

Yet, for all its pitfalls, debt is not an insurmountable obstacle. With the right mindset and a strategic plan of action, it is possible to escape its clutches and reclaim control over our financial destinies. This begins with a willingness to confront our debts head-on, to shine a light on the darkest corners of our financial lives and to confront the demons that lurk within.

In the pages that follow, we'll explore practical strategies for tackling debt and regaining our financial footing. From debt consolidation to budgeting techniques, we'll provide you with the tools and resources you need to break free from the cycle of indebtedness and build a brighter, more secure future for yourself and your loved ones. But more than that, we'll invite you to confront the emotional and psychological toll of debt—to acknowledge the shame and guilt that often accompany financial struggles and to embrace a path of self-compassion and empowerment.

For in the journey towards financial freedom, it is not just our bank accounts that are at stake—it is our very sense of self-worth and dignity. By facing the reality of debt with courage and resilience, we can transform our struggles into opportunities for growth and renewal, paving the way for a future defined not by scarcity and limitation, but by abundance and possibility.

Tracking Your Spending Habits

In the frenetic pace of modern life, it's all too easy to lose sight of where our money is going. From daily coffee runs to impulse purchases and online shopping sprees, our spending habits can quickly spiral out of control if left unchecked. Yet, in order to regain control over our finances, we must first shine a light on the dark corners of our spending habits and confront the patterns that drive our behavior.

This begins with the simple act of tracking our expenses—a task that requires discipline, diligence, and a willingness to confront uncomfortable truths. By meticulously documenting every dollar that flows in and out of our lives, we can gain invaluable insights into our financial habits and identify areas where we may be overspending or misallocating resources.

But tracking our spending isn't just about crunching numbers—it's about cultivating mindfulness and awareness around our financial decisions. It's about pausing to consider the true value and necessity of each purchase and questioning whether it aligns with our long-term goals and priorities. By bringing a sense of intentionality and purpose to our spending, we can begin to make more informed choices that support our financial well-being and align with our values.

In the pages that follow, we'll explore practical strategies for tracking your spending habits and regaining control over your finances. From budgeting apps to spreadsheets and beyond, we'll provide you with the tools and resources you need to monitor your expenses effectively and identify opportunities for savings and optimization. But more than that, we'll invite you to cultivate a deeper understanding of your relationship with money—to explore the emotional and psychological drivers behind your spending habits and to embrace a more mindful and intentional approach to financial management.

For in the journey towards financial freedom, knowledge is power. By tracking your spending habits with rigor and discipline, you can gain valuable insights into your financial behavior and chart a course towards a future defined by abundance and prosperity.

Identifying Your Financial Goals

In the hustle and bustle of daily life, it's all too easy to lose sight of the bigger picture—to get so caught up in the minutiae of everyday existence that we lose sight of our long-term goals and aspirations. Yet, in order to achieve financial freedom and fulfillment, it's essential to have a clear vision of where we're headed and what we hope to accomplish along the way.

This begins with the simple act of identifying our financial goals—a process that requires introspection, reflection, and a willingness to dream big. Whether it's saving for retirement, buying a home, or starting a family, our goals serve as guideposts that help us navigate the complexities of modern finance and stay focused on what truly matters.

But setting goals isn't just about wishful thinking—it's about creating a roadmap for success and taking concrete steps to turn our dreams into reality. This requires breaking down our goals into manageable, actionable steps and developing a strategic plan of attack for achieving them. From setting a budget to establishing a timeline and milestones, each goal represents an opportunity to take control of our financial destiny and shape our future according to our own desires.

In the pages that follow, we'll explore practical strategies for identifying your financial goals and creating a roadmap for success. From SMART goal-setting techniques to visualization exercises and beyond, we'll provide you with the tools and resources you need to clarify your aspirations and chart a course towards a future defined by abundance and prosperity. But more than that, we'll invite you to cultivate a mindset of abundance and possibility—to embrace the belief that anything is possible when we set our sights on what truly matters and commit to taking bold, decisive action.

For in the journey towards financial freedom, our goals serve as beacons of hope and inspiration, guiding us through the darkest of times and propelling us towards a future filled with promise and potential. So join us on this journey as we explore the transformative power of setting goals and chart a course towards a future defined by abundance, prosperity, and fulfillment.

Challenging the Culture of Instant Gratification

In a world where convenience is king and instant gratification reigns supreme, the notion of delayed gratification can feel like a relic of a bygone era. Yet, as we navigate the complexities of modern life, it's becoming increasingly clear that our obsession with immediate satisfaction comes at a steep cost—both to our wallets and our well-being.

At the heart of the culture of instant gratification lies a fundamental truth: our brains are wired to seek out pleasure and avoid pain at all costs. From the earliest days of our evolution, this survival instinct served us well, driving us to pursue sources of sustenance and pleasure with single-minded determination. Yet, in today's hyper-connected world, this same instinct can lead us astray, driving us to make impulsive decisions and prioritize short-term rewards over long-term goals.

Consider, for instance, the allure of credit cards and buy-now-pay-later schemes. By offering the promise of immediate gratification without the need for upfront payment, these financial instruments tap into our primal desire for instant pleasure, luring us into a cycle of debt and financial insecurity. Yet, far from bringing us lasting happiness, this culture of instant gratification only serves to deepen our sense of dissatisfaction and disconnection, leaving us perpetually chasing after the next big thing in a futile quest for fulfillment.

But there is another way. By challenging the culture of instant gratification and embracing the virtues of delayed gratification, we can reclaim control over our impulses and build a future defined by intentionality and purpose. This begins with a willingness to question the narratives that society imposes upon us—to challenge the assumption that happiness can be bought and sold and to recognize that true fulfillment lies not in the accumulation of possessions, but in the pursuit of meaningful experiences and relationships.

In the pages that follow, we'll explore practical strategies for overcoming the allure of instant gratification and cultivating a more mindful and intentional approach to consumption. From setting financial goals to practicing self-discipline and restraint, we'll provide you with the tools and resources you need to break free from the cycle of impulse buying and build a future defined by abundance and prosperity.

But more than that, we'll invite you to challenge the status quo—to question the relentless pursuit of more and to embrace a vision of a future defined not by endless consumption, but by contentment, connection, and fulfillment. For in the journey towards financial freedom, the path to true happiness lies not in the relentless pursuit of instant gratification, but in the patient cultivation of gratitude and the slow, steady pursuit of our deepest aspirations and values.

Embracing Minimalism and Conscious Consumption

In a world awash with abundance, the concept of minimalism may seem like a radical departure from the norm. Yet, as we confront the harsh realities of consumer culture and the toll it exacts on our wallets and our well-being, the virtues of simplicity and restraint are becoming increasingly apparent.

At its core, minimalism is not just about decluttering our physical spaces—it's about decluttering our minds and our lives, freeing ourselves from the relentless pursuit of more and embracing a simpler, more intentional way of living. By prioritizing quality over quantity and experiences over possessions, we can break free from the cycle of mindless consumption and build a future defined by abundance and fulfillment.

But embracing minimalism is more than just a matter of decluttering our closets and downsizing our homes—it's a mindset shift that requires us to question the very foundations of consumer culture and redefine our relationship with material possessions. It's about recognizing that true happiness cannot be bought or sold and that our worth as individuals is not determined by the things we own, but by the depth of our connections and the richness of our experiences.

In the pages that follow, we'll explore practical strategies for embracing minimalism and cultivating a more conscious approach to consumption. From decluttering our physical spaces to reevaluating our spending habits and priorities, we'll provide you with the tools and resources you need to simplify your life and build a future defined by purpose and meaning.

But more than that, we'll invite you to embrace a mindset of abundance—that true wealth lies not in the accumulation of possessions, but in the richness of our experiences and the depth of our connections. For in the journey towards financial freedom, the path to true happiness begins with a willingness to let go of the things that no longer serve us and embrace a simpler, more intentional way of living.

Cultivating Contentment and Gratitude

In a world obsessed with accumulation and excess, the virtues of contentment and gratitude can feel like elusive treasures, forever out of reach. Yet, as we confront the relentless pressures of consumer culture and the toll they exact on our mental and emotional well-being, the importance of cultivating a sense of gratitude and contentment becomes increasingly apparent.

At its core, contentment is not just about being satisfied with what we have—it's about recognizing the abundance that surrounds us and finding joy in the simple pleasures of everyday life. By shifting our focus away from the pursuit of more and embracing a mindset of sufficiency, we can break free from the cycle of comparison and competition and build a future defined by peace and fulfillment.

But cultivating contentment is more than just a matter of mindset—it's a daily practice that requires us to pause, reflect, and appreciate the blessings that abound in our lives. From practicing gratitude journaling to embracing mindfulness and meditation, there are countless ways we can cultivate a sense of contentment and appreciation for the abundance that surrounds us.

In the pages that follow, we'll explore practical strategies for cultivating contentment and gratitude in our lives. From adopting a daily gratitude practice to embracing the principles of mindfulness and simplicity, we'll provide you with the tools and resources you need to break free from the cycle of discontent and build a future defined by peace, purpose, and joy.

But more than that, we'll invite you to embrace a radical vision of abundance—that true wealth lies not in the accumulation of possessions, but in the richness of our relationships and the depth of our connections. For in the journey towards financial freedom, the path to true happiness begins with a willingness to cultivate gratitude for the blessings that abound in our lives and to embrace a mindset of sufficiency and contentment.

Creating a Realistic Budget

In the vast expanse of personal finance, few tools wield as much power or influence as the humble budget. Yet, despite its simplicity and ubiquity, the mere mention of the word can strike fear into the hearts of even the most seasoned financial planners. But fear not, dear reader, for in the pages that follow, we shall demystify the art of budgeting and provide you with the tools and knowledge you need to craft a budget that is not only realistic but empowering.

At its core, a budget is simply a roadmap—a strategic plan of action that helps us navigate the complexities of modern finance and achieve our financial goals. But far from being a rigid set of rules or restrictions, a budget is a flexible and dynamic tool that adapts and evolves with our changing circumstances and priorities. It's about making intentional choices about how we allocate our resources and aligning our spending with our values and aspirations.

But creating a budget isn't just about crunching numbers—it's about cultivating mindfulness and awareness around our financial decisions. It's about pausing to consider the true value and necessity of each expense and questioning whether it aligns with our long-term goals and priorities. By bringing a sense of intentionality and purpose to our spending, we can begin to make more informed choices that support our financial well-being and align with our values.

In the pages that follow, we'll explore practical strategies for creating a realistic budget that works for you. From identifying your income and expenses to setting financial goals and tracking your progress, we'll provide you with the tools and resources you need to take control of your finances and build a future defined by abundance and prosperity.

But more than that, we'll invite you to embrace a mindset of empowerment—that true financial freedom lies not in the absence of constraints, but in the ability to make intentional choices about how we allocate our resources. For in the journey towards financial wellness, the path to success begins with a willingness to take control of our finances and chart a course towards a future filled with possibility and potential.

Managing Debt Effectively

In the labyrinth of personal finance, few specters loom as large or as menacing as the burden of debt. Yet, despite its pervasive presence in our lives, debt is not an insurmountable obstacle—it's a challenge to be confronted and overcome with courage and determination. In the pages that follow, we shall delve into the complexities of debt management and provide you with the tools and knowledge you need to tackle your debts head-on and build a future defined by financial freedom and security.

But before we can embark on this journey, it's essential to confront the stark reality of our debts—to shine a light on the darkest corners of our financial lives and acknowledge the toll that indebtedness exacts on our mental, emotional, and financial well-being. Whether it's credit card balances, student loans, or mortgages, each debt represents a weighty burden that must be acknowledged and addressed if we are to achieve true financial wellness.

But managing debt effectively is more than just a matter of making monthly payments—it's about developing a strategic plan of action that helps us tackle our debts systematically and methodically. From prioritizing high-interest debts to negotiating with creditors and exploring debt consolidation options, there are countless strategies we can employ to accelerate our journey towards debt-free living.

In the pages that follow, we'll explore practical strategies for managing debt effectively and regaining control over your financial destiny. From developing a debt repayment plan to building an emergency fund and exploring alternative income streams, we'll provide you with the tools and resources you need to break free from the shackles of indebtedness and build a future defined by abundance and prosperity.

But more than that, we'll invite you to embrace a mindset of resilience and perseverance—that true financial freedom is not a destination, but a journey. It's about recognizing that setbacks and obstacles are an inevitable part of the process and that success lies not in avoiding them, but in confronting them with courage and determination. For in the journey towards financial wellness, the path to success begins with a willingness to confront our debts head-on and take decisive action to overcome them.

Saving and Investing for the Future

In a world of uncertainty and volatility, few virtues wield as much power or influence as the humble act of saving and investing. Yet, despite its importance in securing our financial future, saving and investing can feel like daunting and complex tasks, fraught with uncertainty and risk. But fear not, dear reader, for in the pages that follow, we shall unravel the mysteries of saving and investing and provide you with the tools and knowledge you need to build a future defined by financial security and abundance.

At its core, saving is simply the act of setting aside a portion of our income for future use—a practice that requires discipline, diligence, and a willingness to delay gratification. But far from being a sacrifice or a burden, saving is an investment in our future selves—a commitment to building a safety net that will protect us in times of need and provide us with the freedom and flexibility to pursue our dreams and aspirations.

But saving is just the first step towards securing our financial future. In order to truly thrive, we must also learn to invest our savings wisely—to put our money to work for us and harness the power of compounding to achieve our long-term financial goals. Whether it's stocks, bonds, real estate, or other asset classes, there are countless investment opportunities available to us, each with its own risks and rewards.

In the pages that follow, we'll explore practical strategies for saving and investing for the future. From setting savings goals to building an investment portfolio and diversifying your assets, we'll provide you with the tools and resources you need to navigate the complexities of the financial markets and build a future defined by prosperity and abundance.

But more than that, we'll invite you to embrace a mindset of abundance and possibility—that true financial freedom is not just about accumulating wealth, but about living a life of purpose and meaning. It's about recognizing that money is a tool that can be used to achieve our goals and aspirations and that our true wealth lies not in our bank accounts, but in the richness of our experiences and the depth of our relationships.

For in the journey towards financial wellness, the path to success begins with a willingness to take control of our finances and build a future defined by possibility and potential. So join us on this journey as we explore the transformative power of saving and investing and chart a course towards a future filled with abundance, prosperity, and fulfillment.

As we continue our exploration of saving and investing for the future, it's essential to delve deeper into the intricacies of building a robust investment portfolio that aligns with your financial goals, risk tolerance, and time horizon. While the prospect of navigating the complexities of the financial markets may seem daunting, rest assured that with the right knowledge and guidance, you can confidently navigate this terrain and build a future defined by financial security and abundance.

One of the fundamental principles of investing is the concept of diversification—a strategy that involves spreading your investments across a variety of asset classes, sectors, and geographic regions to reduce risk and maximize returns. By diversifying your portfolio, you can mitigate the impact of market volatility and ensure that your investments are well-positioned to weather the inevitable ups and downs of the market.

But diversification is just one piece of the puzzle. To truly thrive as an investor, it's essential to develop a deep understanding of the various asset classes available to you and the risks and rewards associated with each. From stocks and bonds to real estate and alternative investments, there are countless options available to investors, each with its own unique characteristics and considerations.

Stocks, for example, represent ownership stakes in companies and offer the potential for significant capital appreciation over time. While stocks historically have provided higher returns than other asset classes, they also come with greater volatility and risk. Bonds, on the other hand, represent loans made to governments or corporations and offer more predictable income streams and lower volatility. By combining stocks and bonds in your portfolio, you can strike a balance between risk and return that aligns with your financial goals and risk tolerance.

Real estate, meanwhile, offers the potential for both income and capital appreciation, making it an attractive option for investors seeking to diversify their portfolios and generate passive income streams. From rental properties to real estate investment trusts (REITs), there are numerous ways to invest in real estate, each with its own unique advantages and considerations.

But perhaps the most important factor to consider when building an investment portfolio is your time horizon—the length of time you expect to hold your investments before needing to access the funds. Investors with longer time horizons can afford to take on more risk and invest in assets with greater potential for growth, whereas those with shorter time horizons may need to prioritize capital preservation and liquidity.

In the pages that follow, we'll explore practical strategies for building a diversified investment portfolio that aligns with your financial goals, risk tolerance, and time horizon. From asset allocation and rebalancing to tax-efficient investing and risk management, we'll provide you with the tools and resources you need to navigate the complexities of the financial markets and build a future defined by prosperity and abundance.

But more than that, we'll invite you to embrace a mindset of empowerment and possibility—that true financial freedom is not just about accumulating wealth, but about living a life of purpose and meaning. It's about recognizing that money is a tool that can be used to achieve our goals and aspirations and that our true wealth lies not in our bank accounts, but in the richness of our experiences and the depth of our relationships.

For in the journey towards financial wellness, the path to success begins with a willingness to take control of our finances and build a future defined by possibility and potential. So join us on this journey as we explore the transformative power of saving and investing and chart a course towards a future filled with abundance, prosperity, and fulfillment.

Dealing with Peer Pressure and Social Expectations

In the age of social media and hyper-connectivity, the pressure to keep up with the Joneses has never been greater. From envy-inducing vacation photos to glamorous party snapshots, we are bombarded with images of perfection and success at every turn, leaving us feeling inadequate and insecure about our own lives. But fear not, dear reader, for in the pages that follow, we shall explore practical strategies for dealing with peer pressure and social expectations and reclaiming control over our financial destinies.

At the heart of peer pressure lies the insidious belief that our worth as individuals is determined by our possessions and accomplishments—that in order to be happy and successful, we must conform to the standards set by society and our peers. But the truth is far more nuanced. True happiness and fulfillment cannot be bought or sold, nor can they be measured by the size of our bank accounts or the brand of our clothes.

Yet, despite our best intentions, the pressure to fit in and conform to societal norms can be overwhelming at times, leading us to make decisions that are not in our best interests. Whether it's splurging on expensive dinners or vacations we can't afford or keeping up with the latest fashion trends, the desire to impress others and gain their approval can cloud our judgment and lead us down a path of financial ruin.

But there is hope. By cultivating a strong sense of self-worth and confidence in our own values and aspirations, we can immunize ourselves against the destructive influence of peer pressure and social expectations. This begins with a willingness to question the narratives that society imposes upon us and to forge our own path based on what truly matters to us.

In the pages that follow, we'll explore practical strategies for dealing with peer pressure and social expectations and staying true to yourself in a world that often demands conformity. From setting boundaries with friends and family to practicing self-care and self-compassion, we'll provide you with the tools and resources you need to navigate the complexities of social dynamics and build a future defined by authenticity and integrity.

But more than that, we'll invite you to embrace a mindset of empowerment and self-confidence—that true happiness and fulfillment come not from seeking validation from others, but from cultivating a deep sense of self-worth and confidence in our own abilities and worthiness. For in the journey towards financial wellness, the path to success begins with a willingness to stand tall in the face of peer pressure and social expectations and forge our own path based on what truly matters to us.

Coping with Emotional Spending Triggers

In the turbulent seas of life, emotions can often serve as powerful catalysts for our actions—guiding us towards pleasure and fulfillment or leading us astray into the depths of despair. Yet, when it comes to our finances, emotions can be both our greatest ally and our most formidable foe, driving us to make impulsive decisions that undermine our long-term financial well-being.

At the heart of emotional spending lies a complex interplay of psychological and emotional factors— ranging from stress and anxiety to boredom and loneliness. Whether it's retail therapy to cope with a bad day at work or impulse purchases to fill the void of emotional emptiness, the urge to spend in response to our emotions can be overwhelming at times, leading us down a path of financial ruin.

But the first step towards overcoming emotional spending is awareness—recognizing the triggers that set off our spending impulses and developing strategies to cope with them effectively. This begins with a willingness to pause and reflect on the underlying emotions driving our spending habits and to question whether our purchases align with our values and long-term goals.

In the pages that follow, we'll explore practical strategies for coping with emotional spending triggers and developing healthier habits around money. From practicing mindfulness and meditation to seeking support from friends and family, we'll provide you with the tools and resources you need to break free from the cycle of emotional spending and build a future defined by financial security and abundance.

But more than that, we'll invite you to embrace a mindset of self-compassion and forgiveness—that true financial wellness comes not from perfection, but from a willingness to acknowledge and learn from our mistakes. For in the journey towards financial freedom, the path to success begins with a willingness to confront our emotional triggers head-on and develop healthier coping mechanisms that support our long-term well-being.

Resisting the Temptation of Impulse Purchases

In a world of instant gratification and endless temptation, the urge to indulge in impulse purchases can be overwhelming at times, leading us to make decisions that are not in our best interests. But fear not, dear reader, for in the pages that follow, we shall explore practical strategies for resisting the temptation of impulse purchases and reclaiming control over our financial destinies.

At the heart of impulse purchasing lies a fundamental truth: our brains are wired to seek out pleasure and avoid pain at all costs. Whether it's the thrill of scoring a bargain or the rush of excitement that comes from owning the latest gadget or fashion trend, the allure of impulse purchases can be irresistible at times, leading us to make decisions that are driven by emotion rather than reason.

But the consequences of giving in to impulse purchases can be significant, leading to financial stress, debt, and regret. That's why it's essential to develop strategies for resisting temptation and making more mindful and intentional choices about how we spend our money.

In the pages that follow, we'll explore practical strategies for resisting the temptation of impulse purchases and developing healthier habits around money. From creating a 24-hour rule for major purchases to unsubscribing from marketing emails and avoiding shopping when hungry or tired, we'll provide you with the tools and resources you need to break free from the cycle of impulse buying and build a future defined by financial security and abundance.

But more than that, we'll invite you to embrace a mindset of empowerment and self-control—that true financial freedom comes not from giving in to our impulses, but from mastering them and making intentional choices that support our long-term well-being. For in the journey towards financial wellness, the path to success begins with a willingness to confront our impulses head-on and develop healthier habits that support our goals and aspirations.

As we delve deeper into the intricacies of resisting the temptation of impulse purchases, it's essential to recognize that overcoming this challenge requires a multifaceted approach that addresses both the external triggers and internal motivations driving our spending habits. While external triggers such as advertising and peer pressure certainly play a significant role in enticing us to make impulsive purchases, it's equally important to acknowledge the internal factors—such as emotions, psychological triggers, and habitual behaviors—that can lead us astray.

One effective strategy for resisting the temptation of impulse purchases is to cultivate mindfulness and awareness around our spending habits. By pausing to reflect on the motivations behind our impulses and questioning whether our purchases align with our values and long-term goals, we can develop a greater sense of clarity and intentionality in our financial decision-making. This may involve implementing a "cooling-off" period before making major purchases, during which we can step back and evaluate whether the purchase is truly necessary or simply driven by momentary desire.

Another key strategy is to create barriers to impulse spending by limiting our exposure to temptation and creating obstacles that make it more difficult to make impulsive purchases. This may involve unsubscribing from marketing emails, avoiding shopping malls and online marketplaces, or setting up automatic savings transfers that reduce the amount of discretionary income available for impulse purchases. By proactively removing ourselves from environments and situations that trigger impulsive spending, we can reduce the likelihood of succumbing to temptation and strengthen our resolve to stick to our financial goals.

Furthermore, developing a clear understanding of our financial values and priorities can help us resist the allure of impulse purchases by providing a guiding framework for our spending decisions. By identifying the things that truly matter to us and aligning our spending with our values and aspirations, we can make more intentional choices about how we allocate our resources and avoid succumbing to the pressure to keep up with external expectations or societal norms. This may involve creating a budget that reflects our values and priorities, setting specific savings goals for things that matter most to us, and regularly reviewing our spending habits to ensure they align with our long-term objectives.

In addition to these proactive strategies, it's also important to develop healthy coping mechanisms for managing stress, boredom, and other emotional triggers that can lead to impulse spending. Rather than turning to shopping as a form of emotional relief or distraction, we can explore alternative ways of addressing our underlying needs and desires—such as exercise, meditation, creative hobbies, or spending time with loved ones. By cultivating healthier outlets for managing our emotions, we can reduce the likelihood of turning to impulsive spending as a coping mechanism and develop more sustainable habits that support our overall well-being.

In the pages that follow, we'll explore these and other practical strategies for resisting the temptation of impulse purchases and reclaiming control over our financial destinies. From cultivating mindfulness and awareness around our spending habits to developing healthy coping mechanisms for managing emotional triggers, we'll provide you with the tools and resources you need to break free from the cycle of impulse buying and build a future defined by financial security and abundance.

But more than that, we'll invite you to embrace a mindset of empowerment and self-control—that true financial freedom comes not from giving in to our impulses, but from mastering them and making intentional choices that support our long-term well-being. For in the journey towards financial wellness, the path to success begins with a willingness to confront our impulses head-on and develop healthier habits that support our goals and aspirations.

Building Healthy Spending Habits

In the pursuit of financial wellness, building healthy spending habits is essential for long-term success. While it may seem daunting at first, developing a conscious and intentional approach to spending can lead to greater financial freedom, security, and peace of mind. In this section, we'll explore practical strategies for building healthy spending habits and making mindful choices that align with your values and goals.

At the core of healthy spending habits lies the principle of mindful consumption—a practice that involves pausing to consider the true value and necessity of each purchase before making it. Rather than succumbing to impulse or emotion-driven spending, mindful consumers take a thoughtful and intentional approach to their purchases, focusing on quality, utility, and long-term satisfaction rather than fleeting gratification.

One effective strategy for building healthy spending habits is to create a budget that reflects your financial goals and priorities. By allocating your income to different categories such as housing, transportation, groceries, and discretionary spending, you can gain a clear understanding of where your money is going and identify areas where you can make adjustments to better align with your values and goals. Additionally, tracking your spending and reviewing your budget regularly can help you stay accountable and identify areas for improvement.

Another key component of healthy spending habits is practicing moderation and restraint when it comes to discretionary expenses. While it's important to enjoy life and treat yourself occasionally, indulging in excessive or frivolous spending can quickly derail your financial goals and lead to unnecessary stress and anxiety. By setting limits on non-essential purchases and prioritizing experiences and relationships over material possessions, you can cultivate a more fulfilling and sustainable approach to spending.

In addition to practicing moderation, it's also important to cultivate gratitude and contentment in your life. Rather than constantly chasing after the next big purchase or material possession, take time to appreciate the blessings and abundance that already exist in your life. Whether it's spending time with loved ones, enjoying nature, or pursuing hobbies and interests, finding fulfillment beyond material possessions can help you break free from the cycle of consumerism and cultivate a more meaningful and fulfilling life.

In the pages that follow, we'll explore these and other practical strategies for building healthy spending habits and making mindful choices that support your financial well-being. From creating a budget and tracking your spending to practicing moderation and cultivating gratitude, we'll provide you with the tools and resources you need to cultivate sustainable lifestyle changes that lead to greater financial freedom, security, and fulfillment.

But more than that, we'll invite you to embrace a mindset of abundance and possibility—that true wealth comes not from the things we own, but from the richness of our experiences and the depth of our relationships. By cultivating healthy spending habits and making mindful choices that align with your values and goals, you can build a future defined by purpose, meaning, and prosperity.

Navigating Consumerism in a Digital Age

In today's hyper-connected world, navigating consumerism has never been more challenging. From targeted advertising and social media influencers to e-commerce giants and digital marketplaces, we are bombarded with messages and temptations to buy at every turn. In this section, we'll explore practical strategies for navigating consumerism in a digital age and making mindful choices that support your financial well-being.

One of the first steps in navigating consumerism in a digital age is to become aware of the tactics and strategies used by marketers and advertisers to influence our behavior. From targeted ads and personalized recommendations to social proof and scarcity tactics, companies employ a wide range of techniques to persuade us to make purchases, often without considering whether we truly need or want the products being promoted.

By developing a critical eye and questioning the messages and narratives presented to us, we can become more discerning consumers and make choices that align with our values and goals. This may involve unsubscribing from marketing emails, limiting your exposure to social media, and avoiding impulse purchases triggered by targeted ads or promotions.

Another key strategy for navigating consumerism in a digital age is to practice mindful consumption and intentional living. Rather than mindlessly scrolling through online marketplaces or adding items to your cart without thinking, take time to pause and consider the true value and necessity of each purchase before making it. Ask yourself whether the product aligns with your values and goals, and whether it will truly enhance your life in a meaningful way.

Additionally, it's important to cultivate a sense of gratitude and contentment in your life. Rather than constantly chasing after the next big purchase or material possession, take time to appreciate the abundance and blessings that already exist in your life. By focusing on experiences and relationships rather than material possessions, you can find fulfillment and happiness beyond the realm of consumerism.

In the pages that follow, we'll explore these and other practical strategies for navigating consumerism in a digital age and making mindful choices that support your financial well-being. From developing a critical eye and questioning marketing messages to practicing mindful consumption and cultivating gratitude, we'll provide you with the tools and resources you need to thrive in a world that often values consumption over contentment.

But more than that, we'll invite you to embrace a mindset of empowerment and self-determination—that true freedom comes not from succumbing to external pressures and influences, but from making conscious choices that align with your values and goals. By navigating consumerism with intentionality and purpose, you can build a future defined by authenticity, fulfillment, and financial well-being.

Finding Fulfillment Beyond Material Possessions

In a world that often equates happiness and success with the accumulation of material possessions, finding fulfillment beyond the realm of consumerism can feel like a radical departure from the norm. Yet, as we confront the harsh realities of modern life and the toll that excessive consumption takes on our planet and our well-being, the importance of cultivating a more meaningful and sustainable approach to living becomes increasingly apparent.

At the heart of finding fulfillment beyond material possessions lies a fundamental truth: true happiness and fulfillment cannot be bought or sold. While material possessions may bring temporary pleasure or satisfaction, they ultimately fail to provide the deep sense of purpose and meaning that comes from living a life aligned with our values and aspirations.

One of the first steps in finding fulfillment beyond material possessions is to cultivate a deep sense of self-awareness and introspection. By reflecting on your values, priorities, and goals, you can gain clarity about what truly matters to you and identify the things that bring you joy and fulfillment. This may involve journaling, meditation, or engaging in meaningful conversations with loved ones to explore your innermost desires and aspirations.

Another key aspect of finding fulfillment beyond material possessions is to prioritize experiences and relationships over material possessions. Rather than focusing on acquiring more stuff, invest your time and energy in activities and pursuits that bring you joy, fulfillment, and a sense of connection with others. Whether it's spending time in nature, pursuing creative hobbies, or volunteering in your community, seek out experiences that enrich your life and deepen your sense of purpose and belonging.

Additionally, it's important to cultivate gratitude and contentment in your life. Rather than constantly striving for more, take time to appreciate the abundance and blessings that already exist in your life. By focusing on what you have rather than what you lack, you can cultivate a sense of gratitude and contentment that transcends the pursuit of material possessions and brings lasting fulfillment and happiness.

In the pages that follow, we'll explore practical strategies for finding fulfillment beyond material possessions and building a life defined by purpose, meaning, and abundance. From cultivating self-awareness and prioritizing experiences to practicing gratitude and contentment, we'll provide you with the tools and resources you need to break free from the cycle of consumerism and build a future defined by authenticity, fulfillment, and financial well-being.

But more than that, we'll invite you to embrace a mindset of possibility and abundance—that true happiness and fulfillment are within reach, not through the acquisition of more stuff, but through the cultivation of meaningful experiences, deep connections, and a sense of purpose that transcends material possessions. By finding fulfillment beyond the realm of consumerism, you can build a future defined by joy, purpose, and lasting fulfillment.

As we continue our exploration of finding fulfillment beyond material possessions, it's essential to delve deeper into the ways in which we can cultivate a more meaningful and purposeful life that transcends the pursuit of material wealth. While the allure of consumerism may be strong, the path to true happiness and fulfillment lies in nurturing our inner selves and investing in experiences and relationships that bring depth and richness to our lives.

One powerful way to find fulfillment beyond material possessions is to cultivate a sense of purpose and meaning in your life. Rather than deriving your sense of worth and identity from external markers of success or status, focus on aligning your actions and choices with your values and aspirations. This may involve setting meaningful goals that reflect your deepest desires and passions, and taking deliberate steps to pursue them with intentionality and dedication.

Additionally, it's important to cultivate a sense of connection and belonging with others. Human beings are inherently social creatures, and our relationships with others play a vital role in shaping our sense of well-being and fulfillment. Whether it's spending quality time with loved ones, participating in meaningful conversations and shared experiences, or supporting others in their time of need, nurturing deep and meaningful connections with others can bring joy, fulfillment, and a sense of belonging that transcends material possessions.

Furthermore, finding fulfillment beyond material possessions involves embracing a mindset of abundance and gratitude. Rather than focusing on what you lack or what others have, cultivate an attitude of gratitude and appreciation for the abundance and blessings that already exist in your life. Take time each day to reflect on the things you are grateful for, whether it's the love and support of friends and family, the beauty of nature, or the simple pleasures of everyday life. By shifting your focus from scarcity to abundance, you can cultivate a sense of contentment and fulfillment that transcends the pursuit of material wealth.

In addition to cultivating purpose, connection, and gratitude, finding fulfillment beyond material possessions also involves embracing a lifestyle of simplicity and minimalism. In a world that often equates success and happiness with the accumulation of stuff, simplifying your life and decluttering your physical and mental space can be a radical act of self-care and liberation. By letting go of excess and focusing on what truly matters, you can create a sense of peace, clarity, and freedom that allows you to fully embrace the present moment and live a life of purpose and meaning.

In the pages that follow, we'll explore practical strategies for finding fulfillment beyond material possessions and building a life defined by purpose, meaning, and abundance. From cultivating purpose and connection to embracing gratitude and simplicity, we'll provide you with the tools and resources you need to break free from the cycle of consumerism and build a future defined by authenticity, fulfillment, and financial well-being.

But more than that, we'll invite you to embrace a mindset of possibility and abundance—that true happiness and fulfillment are within reach, not through the accumulation of more stuff, but through the cultivation of meaningful experiences, deep connections, and a sense of purpose that transcends material possessions. By finding fulfillment beyond the realm of consumerism, you can build a future defined by joy, purpose, and lasting fulfillment.

Stories of Individuals Who Have Successfully Escaped Debt and Consumerism

In this section, we'll delve into the inspiring stories of individuals who have successfully escaped debt and consumerism, demonstrating that financial freedom and fulfillment are achievable goals with determination, perseverance, and the right mindset.

Case Study 1: Sarah's Journey to Financial Freedom

Sarah was like many people living paycheck to paycheck, struggling to make ends meet and drowning in debt. She found herself caught in the vicious cycle of consumerism, constantly seeking fulfillment and validation through material possessions and instant gratification. But deep down, she knew that this lifestyle was unsustainable and ultimately unfulfilling.

Determined to break free from the cycle of debt and consumerism, Sarah embarked on a journey of self-discovery and transformation. She started by taking an honest look at her finances and creating a budget that allowed her to live within her means and prioritize her financial goals. She cut back on non-essential expenses, found ways to increase her income, and started paying off her debts systematically, one step at a time.

But perhaps the most significant change Sarah made was a shift in her mindset. Rather than viewing money as a means to buy happiness, she began to see it as a tool that could be used to create a life of freedom, security, and abundance. She focused on cultivating gratitude and contentment in her life, finding joy in simple pleasures and meaningful experiences rather than material possessions.

Over time, Sarah's efforts began to pay off. As she paid down her debts and built up her savings, she felt a sense of empowerment and liberation that she had never experienced before. She no longer felt the need to keep up with the latest trends or impress others with her possessions. Instead, she focused on living authentically and in alignment with her values, knowing that true happiness and fulfillment could not be bought or sold.

Today, Sarah is debt-free and living a life of financial freedom and abundance. She continues to prioritize her financial goals and make mindful choices about how she spends and saves her money. But more than that, she has found a sense of peace and contentment that transcends the pursuit of material wealth, knowing that true happiness comes from living a life of purpose and meaning.

Case Study: Mark's Journey to Minimalism and Financial Independence

Mark was living the American dream—or so he thought. He had a well-paying job, a big house, a fancy car, and all the trappings of success. But beneath the surface, he felt overwhelmed and unfulfilled by the constant pressure to earn more, buy more, and achieve more. He realized that he was caught in the trap of consumerism, chasing after happiness and fulfillment in all the wrong places.

Determined to break free from the cycle of consumerism and reclaim control over his life, Mark embarked on a journey of minimalism and financial independence. He began by decluttering his physical and mental space, letting go of excess possessions and commitments that no longer served him. He simplified his lifestyle, focusing on the things that truly mattered to him and bringing greater intentionality and purpose to his daily life.

As Mark embraced minimalism, he found that he no longer felt the need to keep up with the Joneses or impress others with his possessions. He discovered a newfound sense of freedom and liberation in living with less, realizing that true happiness and fulfillment could not be found in material possessions but in the richness of experiences and connections with others.

With his newfound clarity and purpose, Mark set ambitious financial goals for himself, including achieving financial independence and retiring early. He lived below his means, saved aggressively, and invested wisely, knowing that every dollar saved brought him one step closer to his dream of financial freedom.

Today, Mark is living proof that it's possible to escape the trap of consumerism and achieve financial independence on your own terms. He has retired early and spends his days pursuing his passions, traveling the world, and giving back to causes he cares about. He has found true happiness and fulfillment in living a life of simplicity, intentionality, and purpose, knowing that the greatest wealth lies not in the accumulation of possessions but in the richness of experiences and relationships.

In the pages that follow, we'll explore more inspiring case studies and success stories of individuals who have successfully escaped debt and consumerism, demonstrating that financial freedom and fulfillment are within reach for anyone willing to take the journey.

Practical Tips and Insights from Real-Life Experiences

In this section, we'll delve deeper into the practical tips and insights gleaned from real-life experiences of individuals who have successfully escaped debt and consumerism. Drawing from their journeys of transformation and growth, we'll uncover actionable strategies and lessons learned that can help you on your own path to financial wellness and fulfillment.

Insight 1: Embrace Minimalism and Conscious Consumption

One of the recurring themes that emerges from the stories of individuals who have successfully escaped debt and consumerism is the importance of embracing minimalism and conscious consumption. By simplifying their lives and focusing on the things that truly matter, they were able to break free from the cycle of excessive consumption and find greater happiness and fulfillment in living with less.

Practical Tip: Start by decluttering your physical and mental space, letting go of possessions and commitments that no longer serve you. Prioritize experiences and relationships over material possessions, and focus on cultivating gratitude and contentment in your life. By adopting a minimalist mindset and embracing conscious consumption, you can free yourself from the burden of excess and create space for what truly matters.

Insight 2: Prioritize Financial Wellness and Independence

Another key insight from the experiences of those who have escaped debt and consumerism is the importance of prioritizing financial wellness and independence. By taking control of their finances and living below their means, they were able to achieve greater security, freedom, and peace of mind.

Practical Tip: Start by creating a budget that reflects your financial goals and priorities, and track your spending to identify areas where you can make adjustments. Prioritize saving and investing for the future, and avoid debt whenever possible. By living within your means and making mindful choices about how you allocate your resources, you can build a solid foundation for financial wellness and independence.

Insight 3: Cultivate a Mindset of Gratitude and Abundance

Finally, one of the most powerful insights from the journeys of those who have escaped debt and consumerism is the importance of cultivating a mindset of gratitude and abundance. By focusing on what they have rather than what they lack, they were able to find greater happiness and fulfillment in their lives.

Practical Tip: Start by practicing gratitude daily, taking time to reflect on the blessings and abundance that already exist in your life. Cultivate contentment and appreciation for the simple pleasures and moments of joy that surround you. By shifting your focus from scarcity to abundance, you can create a more positive and fulfilling outlook on life.

In the pages that follow, we'll continue to explore practical tips and insights from real-life experiences that can help you on your own journey to escaping debt and consumerism. Drawing from the wisdom of those who have walked this path before, we'll provide you with the tools and resources you need to create a future defined by financial wellness, freedom, and fulfillment.

As we delve deeper into the practical tips and insights from real-life experiences of individuals who have successfully escaped debt and consumerism, it becomes evident that there is much to learn from their journeys of transformation and growth. Drawing upon their wisdom, let's explore additional strategies and lessons that can empower you on your own path to financial wellness and fulfillment.

Insight 4: Develop a Long-Term Perspective

One crucial insight gleaned from the experiences of those who have escaped debt and consumerism is the importance of developing a long-term perspective when it comes to financial planning and decision-making. Rather than focusing solely on short-term gratification or immediate desires, they prioritize their long-term goals and aspirations, recognizing that true financial wellness and fulfillment require patience, discipline, and foresight.

Practical Tip: Take time to reflect on your long-term financial goals and aspirations, and develop a plan to achieve them. Set specific, measurable, and achievable goals, and break them down into smaller, actionable steps. By focusing on the big picture and making decisions that align with your long-term objectives, you can create a future defined by financial security and abundance.

Insight 5: Practice Self-Compassion and Resilience

Another valuable insight from the journeys of those who have escaped debt and consumerism is the importance of practicing self-compassion and resilience in the face of setbacks and challenges. Building a strong foundation of self-care and self-acceptance can help you navigate the ups and downs of your financial journey with grace and resilience, empowering you to overcome obstacles and stay focused on your goals.

Practical Tip: Be kind to yourself and practice self-compassion when things don't go as planned. Remember that setbacks are a natural part of any journey, and use them as opportunities for growth and learning. Cultivate resilience by developing healthy coping mechanisms for managing stress and adversity, such as mindfulness, meditation, or seeking support from friends and family. By nurturing your inner resilience, you can weather any storm and emerge stronger and more resilient than ever before.

Insight 6: Seek Support and Accountability

Finally, one of the most powerful insights from the experiences of those who have escaped debt and consumerism is the importance of seeking support and accountability on your journey. Building a network of trusted friends, family members, or mentors who can provide guidance, encouragement, and accountability can make all the difference in staying on track and achieving your financial goals.

Practical Tip: Surround yourself with people who share your values and aspirations, and lean on them for support and encouragement when needed. Consider joining a financial support group or finding a mentor who can provide guidance and accountability on your journey. Share your goals and progress with others, and celebrate your successes together. By building a community of support around you, you can stay motivated and inspired to continue making progress towards your financial goals.

In the pages that follow, we'll continue to explore practical tips and insights from real-life experiences that can empower you on your own journey to escaping debt and consumerism. Drawing from the wisdom of those who have walked this path before, we'll provide you with the tools and resources you need to create a future defined by financial wellness, freedom, and fulfillment.

*

As we continue our exploration of practical tips and insights from real-life experiences, it's important to recognize that the journey to financial wellness and fulfillment is not always easy or straightforward. There will be obstacles and challenges along the way, and it's essential to approach them with patience, resilience, and a willingness to learn and grow.

One valuable lesson we can learn from the experiences of those who have successfully escaped debt and consumerism is the importance of adaptability and flexibility in the face of change. Life is unpredictable, and financial circumstances can shift unexpectedly. By remaining flexible and open to new opportunities and possibilities, you can navigate the twists and turns of your financial journey with grace and resilience.

Practical Tip: Embrace change as an opportunity for growth and transformation, rather than as a setback or obstacle. Stay open to new ideas, perspectives, and possibilities, and be willing to adjust your plans and strategies as needed. Remember that flexibility and adaptability are key to success in any endeavor, and approach each challenge as an opportunity to learn and grow.

Another important insight from the experiences of those who have escaped debt and consumerism is the importance of setting boundaries and priorities in your life. In a world that often values consumption and busyness over contentment and fulfillment, it's essential to prioritize your well-being and focus on the things that truly matter to you.

Practical Tip: Take time to identify your values, priorities, and goals, and set boundaries around your time, energy, and resources accordingly. Learn to say no to activities, commitments, and purchases that don't align with your values or support your goals. By setting clear boundaries and priorities in your life, you can create space for what truly matters and cultivate a greater sense of fulfillment and satisfaction.

In the pages that follow, we'll continue to explore practical tips and insights from real-life experiences that can empower you on your own journey to escaping debt and consumerism. Drawing from the wisdom of those who have walked this path before, we'll provide you with the tools and resources you need to create a future defined by financial wellness, freedom, and fulfillment.

Taking Control of Your Financial Future

In this final section, we'll explore the key steps you can take to take control of your financial future and embark on a journey towards greater freedom, security, and fulfillment.

Step 1: Cultivate Financial Awareness

The first step in taking control of your financial future is to cultivate awareness around your financial situation. Take time to assess your income, expenses, debts, and savings, and create a clear picture of your financial health. Track your spending habits, identify areas where you can make adjustments, and set specific goals for yourself based on your values and priorities.

Step 2: Create a Plan

Once you have a clear understanding of your financial situation, it's time to create a plan for achieving your goals. Set realistic and achievable targets for yourself, whether it's paying off debt, saving for retirement, or building an emergency fund. Break down your goals into smaller, actionable steps, and develop a timeline for achieving them. Remember to review and adjust your plan regularly as your circumstances change.

Step 3: Prioritize Financial Wellness

Make financial wellness a priority in your life by adopting healthy spending habits, practicing moderation, and living within your means. Avoid unnecessary debt and impulse purchases, and prioritize saving and investing for the future. Consider automating your savings and retirement contributions to ensure consistency and discipline in your financial habits.

Step 4: Build Resilience

Financial resilience is essential for weathering life's ups and downs and staying on track towards your goals. Build an emergency fund to cover unexpected expenses, and consider diversifying your income streams to reduce reliance on any single source of income. Develop healthy coping mechanisms for managing stress and uncertainty, and seek support from friends, family, or financial professionals when needed.

Step 5: Invest in Yourself

Investing in yourself is one of the most important investments you can make for your future. Take time to develop your skills, knowledge, and abilities, and invest in education and training opportunities that will enhance your earning potential and career prospects. Prioritize your physical and mental well-being, and cultivate healthy habits that support your overall health and happiness.

By taking control of your financial future and committing to sustainable change, you can build a life defined by freedom, security, and fulfillment. Remember that financial success is not about how much you earn or how many possessions you have, but about living in alignment with your values and priorities and creating a future that brings you joy and satisfaction.

Committing to Sustainable Change

In this final section, we'll explore the importance of committing to sustainable change and taking concrete steps towards building a future defined by financial wellness, freedom, and fulfillment.

Step 6: Embrace a Mindset of Growth

Committing to sustainable change requires a mindset of growth and resilience. Embrace challenges as opportunities for growth and learning, and approach setbacks as temporary obstacles on your journey towards success. Cultivate self-awareness and self-compassion, and celebrate your progress and accomplishments along the way.

Step 7: Stay Focused and Motivated

Stay focused and motivated by keeping your goals front and center in your mind. Visualize your ideal future and the life you want to create for yourself, and use that vision as motivation to stay committed to your goals. Surround yourself with positive influences and supportive individuals who encourage and inspire you to be your best self.

Step 8: Practice Patience and Persistence

Building a life of financial wellness and fulfillment takes time and effort, so practice patience and persistence as you work towards your goals. Stay committed to your plan, even when progress feels slow or setbacks occur. Remember that every step forward, no matter how small, brings you closer to your ultimate destination.

Step 9: Celebrate Your Successes

Take time to celebrate your successes and milestones along the way. Acknowledge and appreciate the progress you've made, and celebrate the achievements, no matter how small. Reward yourself for reaching your goals and milestones, and use these moments of celebration as fuel to keep you motivated and inspired on your journey.

By committing to sustainable change and taking concrete steps towards building a future defined by financial wellness, freedom, and fulfillment, you can create a life that brings you joy, satisfaction, and abundance. Remember that change is a process, and that every step you take towards your goals brings you closer to the life you've always dreamed of.

In the pages that follow, we've explored practical strategies and insights from real-life experiences that can empower you on your journey towards financial wellness and fulfillment. From cultivating mindfulness and intentionality in your spending habits to embracing minimalism and prioritizing experiences over possessions, we've provided you with the tools and resources you need to take control of your financial future and build a life that brings you joy and satisfaction.

But more than that, we've invited you to embrace a mindset of possibility and abundance—that true happiness and fulfillment are within reach, not through the accumulation of possessions or the pursuit of external validation, but through the cultivation of meaningful experiences, deep connections, and a sense of purpose that transcends material wealth.

As you embark on your journey towards financial wellness and fulfillment, remember that you are not alone. Seek support and guidance from friends, family, or financial professionals, and surround yourself with positive influences that encourage and inspire you to be your best self. Stay committed to your goals, stay focused on your vision, and stay true to yourself as you navigate the twists and turns of your financial journey.

With determination, resilience, and a willingness to embrace change, you can create a future defined by financial wellness, freedom, and fulfillment—a future where you are empowered to live life on your own terms and pursue your passions and dreams with confidence and joy.

Resources and Further Reading

In this final section, we'll provide you with a curated list of recommended books, websites, and tools for financial education and support. These resources cover a wide range of topics, from budgeting and saving to investing and retirement planning, and are designed to empower you on your journey towards financial wellness and fulfillment.

Books

1. "The Total Money Makeover" by Dave Ramsey: This bestselling book offers a step-by-step plan for getting out of debt and achieving financial freedom. Ramsey's straightforward approach to money management has helped millions of people take control of their finances and build wealth for the future.

2. "Your Money or Your Life" by Vicki Robin and Joe Dominguez: This classic book offers a holistic approach to personal finance, emphasizing the connection between money and fulfillment. Through practical exercises and insights, Robin and Dominguez show readers how to align their spending with their values and create a life of financial independence and meaning.

3. "Rich Dad Poor Dad" by Robert T. Kiyosaki: In this groundbreaking book, Kiyosaki shares the lessons he learned from his "rich dad" and "poor dad" about money and wealth. Through entertaining anecdotes and practical advice, Kiyosaki challenges conventional wisdom about money and offers readers a new perspective on building wealth and achieving financial success.

4. "The Millionaire Next Door" by Thomas J. Stanley and William D. Danko: This eye-opening book explores the habits and behaviors of America's wealthy elite and reveals surprising insights about what it takes to accumulate wealth. Through in-depth research and interviews, Stanley and Danko identify the

key traits and characteristics that distinguish millionaires from the average person and offer practical advice for building wealth over time.

5. "Broke Millennial: Stop Scraping By and Get Your Financial Life Together" by Erin Lowry: Geared towards millennials, this accessible and engaging book offers practical advice for managing money and building wealth in the modern world. From budgeting and saving to investing and retirement planning, Lowry covers all the essentials of personal finance and empowers readers to take control of their financial futures.

Websites

1. Investopedia (www.investopedia.com): Investopedia is a comprehensive resource for investing education, financial news, and market analysis. Whether you're a beginner or an experienced investor, Investopedia offers a wealth of articles, tutorials, and resources to help you make informed decisions about your finances.

2. NerdWallet (www.nerdwallet.com): NerdWallet is a popular personal finance website that offers tools and advice for managing money, comparing financial products, and making smart financial decisions. From credit cards and banking to investing and insurance, NerdWallet provides unbiased reviews and recommendations to help you navigate the complexities of personal finance.

3. The Balance (www.thebalance.com): The Balance is a trusted source for personal finance advice and information, covering topics ranging from budgeting and saving to investing and retirement planning. With a team of expert writers and editors, The Balance offers clear and concise articles and resources to help you achieve your financial goals.

4. Mint (www.mint.com): Mint is a free online budgeting and personal finance tool that helps you track your spending, set financial goals, and manage your money more effectively. With Mint, you can create a customized budget, monitor your accounts and transactions, and receive personalized insights and recommendations to improve your financial health.

5. Personal Capital (www.personalcapital.com): Personal Capital is a comprehensive financial planning platform that offers tools and services for managing your investments, tracking your net worth, and planning for retirement. With Personal Capital, you can sync all of your financial accounts in one place, analyze your portfolio's performance, and receive

personalized advice and recommendations from certified financial planners.

Tools

1. YNAB (You Need a Budget) (www.youneedabudget.com): YNAB is a popular budgeting app that helps you take control of your finances and achieve your financial goals. With YNAB, you can create a customized budget, track your spending in real-time, and prioritize your money based on your values and priorities.

2. Acorns (www.acorns.com): Acorns is a micro-investing app that helps you save and invest your spare change automatically. With Acorns, you can round up your everyday purchases to the nearest dollar and invest the difference in a diversified portfolio of ETFs. It's a simple and convenient way to start investing for the future without even thinking about it.

3. Betterment (www.betterment.com): Betterment is an online investment platform that offers personalized investment advice and portfolio management services. With Betterment, you can set financial goals, build a customized investment portfolio, and receive ongoing guidance and support from certified financial planners.

4. TurboTax (www.turbotax.intuit.com): TurboTax is a popular tax preparation software that helps you file your taxes quickly and accurately. With TurboTax, you can easily import your financial information, maximize your deductions and credits, and file your taxes electronically for a fast and hassle-free experience.

5. Credit Karma (www.creditkarma.com): Credit Karma is a free online service that helps you monitor your credit score and report, track your credit history, and improve your financial health. With Credit Karma, you can access your credit scores from TransUnion and Equifax, receive personalized recommendations for improving your credit, and stay informed about changes to your credit report.

By exploring these recommended books, websites, and tools for financial education and support, you can gain the knowledge and confidence you need to take control of your financial future and build a life of freedom, security, and fulfillment. Remember that financial wellness is a journey, not a destination, and that every step you take towards greater financial empowerment brings you one step closer to the life you've always dreamed of.

www.ingramcontent.com/pod-product-compliance
Lightning Source LLC
Chambersburg PA
CBHW050033260726
48658CB00005B/1589